A D H D
A DISORDER HIDDEN DEEP

OWEN WILLIAMS (ELEMENTOG)

Grosvenor House
Publishing Limited

This book is published by
Grosvenor House Publishing Ltd
Link House
140 The Broadway, Tolworth, Surrey, KT6 7HT.
www.grosvenorhousepublishing.co.uk

A CIP record for this book
is available from the British Library

Paperback ISBN 978-1-83615-582-9
eBook ISBN 978-1-83615-583-6

My son was born on March 24, 2010, six weeks earlier than his expected due date. For those unfamiliar with the term "premature", it refers to a birth that occurs three to four weeks prior to the typical 37-week gestation period, which can result in the child's organs and body not being fully developed. This was true in my son's case.

Being a full-time parent presents its own challenges, and the additional stress of my son's ADHD was not something that had been identified from birth, in fact I did not suspect or had any reason to believe that he had any symptoms or shown any signs or spectrum disorders. But, to be honest, I was so un educated on ADHD that even if he did, I didn't know what I was looking out for so I never had no real understanding of what age he might have developed this disorder from. In fact it was really brought to my attention through his ages of one to four. I had sleepless nights where he cried for nights consistently, even after being washed, clothed, bottle-fed. He seemed unrested and unsettled and his behaviour was unpredictable. At times he would throw his bottle across the room and then cry for me to come and pick it up and give it back to him while he was in his cot. He would bite when upset, he would act out for attention when I was occupied with tasks such as cooking and sought constant physical interaction but nothing out the ordinary for me to think this wasn't the norm of every child at that age.

It wasn't until he started attending nursery at the age of four. It was noticeable that he had a speech impermanent, and his speech was noticeably delayed. I feel this contributed to his frustration and outbursts, also he would push over other students and lash out as a means of communication. His behaviour was hyperactive then very unpredictable, so I was advised by his class teacher at the time to go and have him assessed for ADHD and autism. Plus, at the age of four, he was still pointing and humming to identify things around him. Various classroom staff observed that he also had struggles with social interactions unlike his other peers who

could articulate clear words and form complete sentences, and seem to be a lot more content in the same environment.

I first consulted a doctor to have him evaluated, but since he was only four at the time, I was advised to wait until he turned five years old where they could undergo a full assessment. This recommendation came from a paediatrician as diagnosing ADHD requires the child to display symptoms across various settings and surroundings including home, school, school trips and other social environments. My son began to demonstrate these at home; he would become restless when you could see it was from the day's events where he had literally used up all his energy. It would make him really emotionally because he wasn't getting the sleep he was requiring.

I found that his behaviour was much more challenging when he was away from me, like at school he would display behaviours that he wasn't really displaying at home. I learnt ADHD/autism has different forms and types on the spectrum so it was important for me to understand my son's.

In, my quest to gain a better understanding, I would make notes of times he ate, I would write down the times where he seemed happy, and how he occupied his time – as in what his interests and hobbies were. I would keep a daily log of his routine to understand his patterns. In my quest for understanding I read numerous books and consulted various specialists regarding the causes of ADHD, potential triggers and effective strategies for nurturing a child which this condition.

The prevailing recommendation for managing ADHD was medication. While medication is effective for many it does not yield the same results for all children, particularly for those children that are born prematurely as was the case with my son.

There were times when I felt exhausted, as his increasingly challenging and unpredictable behaviour demanded more of my attention and determination. It wasn't until he was five that he was eventually seen by a paediatrician and put onto a waiting list alongside many other young children to await evaluation. I was told that the evaluation would not happen with immediate effect but I would be informed by post once an appointment date could be generated – this was anything from one to three years which was not what I was expecting but I was just relieved that he was on the wating list so that he could have his needs met and supported respectfully. I had been informed that same day that there was a backlog which they were trying to deal with as quickly as possible, so I had a letter of apology for the congestion.

Eventually, after his sixth birthday, he was given an appointment and seen by a paediatrician, and this was my candid observation.

I recall attending the initial assessment where the paediatrician conducted a series of exercises. These including having my son walk in a straight line, balance on one leg, pick up cutlery, throw and kick a football, and engage in various activities involving evaluating his speech and his pronunciations and responses to certain words such as no, yes, well done, good boy, that's not nice, hello, goodbye, please, thank you.

A couple months after the evaluation, my son was referred to a speech and language therapist and was diagnosed with dyspraxia, ADHD, and autism. During his speech and language therapy sessions, the focus was on improving his pronunciation of words and single syllables. I found the observation and the experience both enlightening and beneficial. I felt as if I learnt so much myself by just attending and trying to take in as much information as I could for my own understanding of the methods that significantly aided my son's speech development. I incorporated many of the techniques learned during the assessments into our daily routine at home.

METHODS/TECHNIQUES

1. Abundance of praise. Whenever he achieved anything positive or displayed good behaviour at school, I would provide abundance of praise through stickers or reward charts acknowledging his efforts, like cleaning and keeping his room tidy. Not only did I find that it conveyed acceptance and appreciation, but it also helped enhance his social skills and fostered an unimaginable level of self-confidence. Furthermore, it promoted positive emotions within my son.

2. Not raising my voice, even in instances of wrongdoing. Resorting to shouting, I found, was counterproductive. It alienated my son and prevented him from absorbing the intended message. I felt that I myself had to learn , realise and understand how crucial mastering the ability of calmness was, especially when it came to addressing behaviour discipline. I quickly learnt to engage in a firm and fair discussion, and little things like bringing myself to his height level when I was addressing him. I asked him questions like, "That's not nice is it, do you think that was acceptable behaviour? "What do we say when we are wrong?" {"Sorry"}. I found this method made him have a better understanding of why he was being addressed, and I felt it brought out a more favourable outcome than towering over him and shouting about his behaviour. It took a considerate amount of time, patience and repetition of the same strategies before we began to see positive change.

3. Never result to physical punishment, as this only breeds confusion and resentment. Such actions hinder the development of mutual understanding between me, being the parent, and the child, and mindfully understanding that the child may internalise this behaviour and replicate it towards others as a form of observational learning. That's why studies show that the most detrimental response to a child's behaviour is physical abuse in both sexes.

According to a researched abstract by Allison M Briscoe-Smith, Child Abuse Negl. 2007 Nov 1, not only young boys but 14% of 140 girls with ADHD and 4.5% of 85 girls without ADHD between the ages of six and twelve had suffered physical abuse in some way. A different perspective on the influence of traumatic stress on ADHD and general well-being can be gained by examining the research surrounding adverse childhood experiences (ACEs). ACEs refer to distressing and traumatic incidents that take place prior to the age of 18, which can adversely affect an individual's physical, social and emotional health. These experiences encompass, but are not limited to, the points below:

- Abuse

- Psychological

- Sexual

- Neglect

- Physical

- Emotional

Living with a child with ADHD/autism and dyspraxia

I found that a hug and expressing the words "I love you" served as a powerful remedy for managing my son's emotions related to ADHD, bringing to light how significantly important emotional support was. Some individuals may choose a different approach and distance themselves from such responsibilities, concentrating instead on the adverse effects and succumbing to the anxiety associated with managing such a disorder. In contrast, I opted for a proactive approach, addressing ADHD with compassion and attentiveness.

Initially I sought to comprehend the various spectrums and triggers involved, aiming to establish an appropriate equilibrium. To facilitate this, it took a lot of mental time and exhaustion as I felt I was always overthinking of what to do next. I spoke to various parents and individuals that had either experienced living with a sibling with ADHD/autism or had a child who was diagnosed with the spectrums/disorders and here in their own words are some of the main challenges they faced and the experiences and difficulties that they endured!

I orchestrated and engaged in a conversation with my friend about her experiences as a parent with a child on the ADHD spectrum.

'TRIXSY' from London said, "My daughter had ADHD and at times it made me feel like I didn't want to be in this world. I could not cope with the anger, her abuse, like smashing up my house, I had police coming to the house once a day. I cried for days as I didn't know how to cope with her needs especially the fact that I had other children that needed my attention and love and I felt that I was always putting my daughter's ADHD needs first over everything, at times, even myself. But as time has gone on, and she has developed a routine and grew older, things have improved massively but it's still very hard."

'CJ' from Birmingham said, "My daughter is still only two years old and is still waiting to be assessed for ADHD and ASD. It can be quite challenging at times since she can be very affectionate and very spiteful. She struggles a lot at school, particularly with making friends; she is always very energetic and in people's faces, loud, yet she dislikes it when others are loud. It can be tough because she hasn't been diagnosed yet because of her age, and people don't understand why she behaves the way she does. At school she often gets singled out because they lack enough trained staff to recognise and support her needs."

My son developed a strong preference for maintaining the arrangement of things in his bedroom, finding comfort in their familiar placement and doing everything from getting dressed to having breakfast to how he started his day in a particular order. Even a sudden change in his teacher at school necessitated prior notification to help him prepare for the unexpected, particularly not knowing if it would cause him to feel uneasy in the classroom.

According to an article in *Child Mind Institute* written by Katherine Martinelli, "Why do kids have trouble with transition?", Michael Rosenthal PhD, a clinical neuropsychologist, explains in a study how children on the autistic spectrum have hyper-focused interests and a preference for performing the same tasks in the same order. This is referred to as cognitive inflexibility. When a child with autism is faced with sudden changes or transitions, according to Michael Rosenthal, children with ADHD struggle to manage their emotions more than other children, the wiring in the brain centres that are involved in helping kids exercise control over their emotions are less developed, so you get bigger emotional displays from them compared to kids who don't have ADHD.

Covid-19 had a profound effect on the quality of life and well-being of children with ADHD/autism. A study conducted in Brazil revealed that 63% of children exhibited signs of sadness, irritability, depression and sleep disturbances during the quarantine period. New behaviours emerged daily, with 43% of children displaying increased agitation. Following the Covid quarantine, these same individuals demonstrated a significant reduction in irritability and agitation, decreasing to 15% and 20%, respectively; however, instances of sadness saw a slight increase. At the height of the pandemic, 52% of children experienced sleep issues, anxiety, and unpredictable behaviours, with insomnia rates rising to 31% after the lockdown concluded. A follow-up study on the same group indicated that only 4% reported ongoing sleep difficulties and unpredictable behaviour patterns. ADHD is associated with an increased likelihood of developing conduct disorders related to social behaviour. This group of children tends to have a higher incidence of interactions with law enforcement and the criminal justice system. A comprehensive understanding of ADHD may influence the outcomes related to criminal activities including the necessity for referrals, charges, or incarceration.

INTERNET GAMING DISORDER

Internet gaming disorder, also referred to as gaming disorder, has been the subject of extensive research, particularly in South Korea. Studies indicate that approximately 15-25% of children and adolescents are affected. Furthermore, individuals exhibiting symptoms associated with ADHD are found to have a significantly elevated prevalence of gaming disorder. Research indicates that those diagnosed with gaming disorder also show higher rates of ADHD symptoms.

I feel like I can relate to this as my son spent a lot of time engaging and seemed to find comfort in online gaming. Not only did he seem to be engrossed and fixated with concentration, at times he seemed socially detached from the rest of the house and he only seemed to engage when it was dinner time or when he was called, which often required me calling numerous times before I would finally get a response. I established a new routine in my home that prohibited the use of gadgets, phones, or online gaming after 8pm on school nights, coinciding with bedtime. I believed that allowing my son access to the internet while being alone in his room could lead to negatives effects, so I restricted computer access to weekends (Saturday and Sunday) providing that school behaviour was satisfactory, and all assignments were completed. I felt it was crucial to enforce this immediately because I could see an emerging gaming addiction, and I wanted to prevent him from developing habits that would be difficult to break and, as the parent, it was my duty to create a healthy balance at home.

Indicators of gaming-related issues include feelings of fatigue and disconnection, difficulties in maintaining focus in educational settings, placing gaming above other pursuits, and challenges in face-to-face social interactions. While video games can activate the brain in a manner akin to stimulants such as amphetamines and methylphenidate, they may also adversely impact the mental well-being of children.

There is often confusion regarding the distinction between ADHD and behaviours associated with high intelligence. Opinions on this matter vary widely, as the disorder encompasses a range of manifestations. It is essential to comprehend the unique characteristics of each child within this spectrum. ADHD may serve as an underlying factor for other syndromes. Some individuals view children with ADHD as possessing significant potential, conversely, autism is often perceived as a developmental delay in cognitive function.

Concerns have been raised about the potential link between MMR vaccines and the onset of autism. A considerable number of parents choose to forgo vaccinations for their children, fearing that these immunisations may trigger or contribute to autism. The BCG vaccine, while also subject to scrutiny, is administration to prevent tuberculosis and other related conditions. This vaccine was developed for children in the 1970s. Many people hold varying opinions on whether autism is a condition that has been artificially created, as it was not widely recognised in the 1970s and certainly was not as prevalent as it is today.

I believe that if I had been informed about my ADHD/autism when my child was just a few months old, my perspective on vaccinations might have changed, perhaps I would have conducted more research before proceeding with them. Additionally, I learned that unvaccinated children could struggle to secure a nursery position or even face exclusion from school, which was something I wanted to avoid for my son. I was only a single dad too, so I was grateful for the additional support at the time. An article by *immunize.org*, "What if you don't vaccinate your child?", highlights the importance of how a child not being fully vaccinated can affect them in their communities, schools, and prevent them catching from various other diseases/infections.

It wasn't until my son was about seven that I also started to realise that he had difficulty holding item such as a knife, fork, and spoon. At dinner time I would try to encourage him to hold his cutlery the right way, but the more I tried the more he became more frustrated and resorted back to a way that was more comfortable for him. Sometimes I would often give up trying to show him as he would become increasingly and visibly upset, plus the main objective was for him to eat all his dinner before it got cold, which he managed, but dinner times possessed many challenges.

He eventually received cutlery holders from the paediatrician, which assisted him in gripping items like cutlery more effectively, and I observed significant enhancements in his ability to handle his utensils resulting in less frustration during mealtimes. I felt tremendous relief, as one of my primary worries was how he would be perceived by his classmates while eating his lunch at school. Fortunately, with regular practice with the holders and demonstrating to him how I use my cutlery, since children often imitate their parents, he made such progress that by the age of ten, he no longer required or felt the need to use the cutlery holders. I kept them away in a safe place in case they were ever needed again. I was so proud of my son and happy that he had overcome an obstruction that at first seemed to only look to be getting more complicated, and that taught me that he had a determination to succeed.

Eventually, after months of waiting and countless assessments, my son was finally prescribed methylphenidate medication.

MEDICATION

METHYLPHENIDATE (methylphenidate is a stimulant that treats attention deficit/hyperactivity disorder (ADHD). It works by improving your focus and reducing impulsive behaviours. Prior to his medication, I believed that engaging in activities like swimming, playing football, visiting the park to use the swings, riding his bike and feeding the ducks at the lake, and replaced his gaming time with baking and helping prepare dinner with little tasks like cutting vegetables, which significantly contributed to my son's growth. Channelling his energy into these productive pursuits appeared to have a beneficial impact. I noticed it also aided in enhancing his communication abilities and taught him how to engage with others in society, which was crucial. I sat with the doctor and he explain how treating ADHD with medication is successful and supported by research and treating ADHD in autistic individuals with medication also helps to alleviate its symptoms. However, what I found during research is the ADHD medication won't lessen the characteristics of autism and arguably other help could be required and I feel that this is very important to know and understand.

METHYLPHENIDATE TABLETS

Before taking this medication, your doctor should be informed of the following:

- Anxiety or panic attacks

- Issues with circulation in your fingers and toes

- Glaucoma

- Arterial hardening or blockage or heart vessel problems

- A history of heart disease or any heart defects

- High blood pressure

- A history of drug or alcohol abuse

- A history of stroke

- Liver disease

- Any mental health issues

- Motor tics, or a family history or diagnosis of Tourette's syndrome

- Seizures

- Thoughts, plans, or attempts of suicide, a previous suicide attempt by you or a family member

- Thyroid disease

- Any unusual or allergic reactions to methylphenidate, other medications, foods dues or preservatives

- Currently pregnant or attempting to become pregnant

- Breastfeeding

What adverse effects might I encounter from this medication? Side effects that you should promptly inform your doctor about include:

- Allergic reactions – skin rash, itching, hives swelling of the face, lips tongue, or throat

- Changes in heart rhythm – rapid or irregular

- Heartbeat, dizziness, feeling faint or lightheaded

- Chest pain, difficulty breathing. Elevated blood pressure

- Alterations in mood and behaviour – anxiety

- Nervousness, confusion, hallucinations, irritability, hostility, thoughts of suicide or self-harm. Worsening mood, feelings of depression, prolonged or painful erections

- Raynaud phenomenon – cool, numb or painful fingers or toes that may change colour from pale to blue to red

- Stroke in adults – sudden numbness or weakness in the face, arm, or leg. Difficulty speaking, confusion, trouble walking, loss of balance or coordination, dizziness, severe headache, or changes in vision

How should I administer this medication?

Take this medication orally with a glass of water. Adhere to the instructions on the prescription label. It is recommended to take this medication 30 to 45 minutes prior to meals. Unless your doctor advises otherwise, ensure that you take your medication at consistent intervals. Generally, the final dose of the day should be taken at least four to six hours before going to sleep to avoid disrupting your rest. Do not take your medication more frequently than prescribed.

'CHARMAINE' from Birmingham said, "My son is now 18 years old and has autism (Asperger's). I realised he was different from early age; as a baby, he would often cry late at night, and the only way to soothe him was by taking him to the window to look outside. His food preferences were quite limited, primarily consisting of pizza, carrots, chicken nuggets, and cucumber. The primary school staff dismissed my concerns, claiming he was fine, but his struggles became evident in senior school where they quickly recognised the challenges he faced. He was then evaluated and officially diagnosed. Unfortunately, he didn't receive significant help in school or the support he required. He is an emotional young man who takes things very personally. There seems to be little support for parents and friends I speak with that have faced similar situations if not the same experiences. Now he is currently having difficulty finding a job as there is again limited assistance available for young adults with autism seeking employment. I would love to see increased support and resources for all young adults with autism seeking job opportunities."

Attention deficit hyperactivity disorder (ADHD) is frequently perceived negatively as a collection of difficult symptoms. Nevertheless, numerous highly accomplished individuals credit their success to their ADHD, at times it is even referred to as a superpower. Here are several characteristics that often enable individuals with ADHD to thrive:

- Intense focus

- Great passion

- Perseverance and motivation

- Willingness to take risks

- Positive outlook

- Creative thinking

Successful TV personalities / musicians / business people with ADHD/autism spectrum disorders

According to a study in ADHD Centre, UK specialist in private assessments and treatment for ADHD, Chatham House, CC BY 2.0. via Wikimedia Commons, several well-known figures with ADHD have embraced these traits and reached remarkable success in their respective fields. Business leaders among the prominent high-achieving entrepreneurs with ADHD are Richard Branson, Bill Gates and Walt Disney to name a few.

Richard Branson learned to channel his unique talents and creativity; he went on to create an extraordinary business empire. He is recognised as one of the most successful and renowned entrepreneurs of contemporary times.

Bill Gates, the co-founder of Microsoft, is recognised for having ADHD and has openly discussed facing challenges related to its symptoms. He is also among the richest individuals globally. When he left Harvard to launch Microsoft, remarkably he had already been working on computer programming for several years and had even designed a scheduling system for his high school while he was still a student.

Walt Disney is believed to have exhibited signs of ADHD and left school at an early age. Subsequently, he established the Disney empire. Certainly, having entrepreneurial ADHD doesn't guarantee notoriety, yet examples are abundant, and confidence in oneself and a clear vision appear to be fundamental for achieving success. According to the article in the ADHD Centre, "Successful people with ADHD Superpowers", a famous quote from Walt Disney was, "Every one of our dreams can become a reality if we possess the bravery to chase them."

What fascinated me about all three successful entrepreneurs was that they all had an element of risk-taking, drive, imaginative and shared an inner self-belief and passion, and did not let ADHD defined them. I think it is so important for others to realise that it all depends on mindset and how you look at the symptoms and how you go about assisting people on the spectrum. As we see, Bill Gates, Richard Branson, and Walt Disney all went on to become very successful in their respected fields and continue to show that even with different challenges of ADHD, you can still achieve your dreams.

Several prominent actors and television figures have been candid about their experiences with ADHD. Paris Hilton, the hotel heiress, reality tv personality, socialite, entrepreneur, singer and actress, was diagnosed with ADHD during her childhood. In a recent documentary focused on ADHA, she shared, "I believe it provides me with the motivation and advantage necessary for success. When properly supported, it can function as a superpower."

Grammy award recipient, Solange Knowles, received an ADHD diagnosis on two occasions – initially, she was sceptical about it. "I had a theory that ADHD was merely a fabricated condition to profit from medication, but the second physician confirmed my diagnosis," she shared with *Blackdoctor.org*. Historically, ADHD has been perceived as a condition predominately affecting males, with the assumption that they represented most cases. However, new studies are increasingly examining the impact of the disorder females, allowing for earlier identification of ADHD in women's lives. The passionate singer expressed that she has always been brimming with energy and asserts that her occasional rapid speech and lively demeanour have made some think she was using drugs when the actual reason was ADHD. While ADHD/autism may present certain challenges, numerous individuals with ADHD/ autism achieve great success in their lives like Solange.

Former Spice Girl and singer, Mel B, utilises nature and physical activity to manage her anxiety and ADHD symptoms. From a page in a recent article titled "Successful people with ADHD superpowers", she goes on to say, "Working out allows me to meditate and alleviate, it enables me to concentrate on myself for that one hour."

Amongst many other TV personalities, Zayn Malik, a former member of One Direction, was identified as having ADHD during his childhood. He went on to say, in his autobiography titled *Zayn*, "As a child, I was quite unruly. I struggled to concentrate and had difficulty managing the direction of my thoughts. I was always finding myself in trouble."

Referring to the same article, under the title "athletes", it's estimated that around 8-10% of professional athletes have on the ADHD spectrum. Individuals with ADHD possess incredible drive, determination, energy, and focus. Consequently, a significant number of elite athletes are believed to have this condition.

Michael Phelps is the swimmer with the most Olympic medals in history, boasting an astounding 23 gold medals. He serves as an inspiration for those with ADHD, proving that it can be overcome! He said, "Challenges will arise. People will question you. Errors will happen. However, with dedication there are no boundaries."

Overthinking

I frequently found myself pondering how many other parents with children on the autism/ADHD spectrum were managing and I could only empathise with them, recognizing the challenges I encountered with my son, who was also born premature. This is why it was essential for me to gather perspectives from other parents and for them to share their stories, allowing not only me but those who are in or have been in similar situations to find solace in knowing they are not alone. Many times I felt as though I was the only one facing these challenges with my son, but upon research and speaking to others and listening to others' stories and being able to relate, I was able to come to a better understanding. Despite the initial difficulty in grasping the nuances of the spectrums, I was determined not to let it define my son or limit his dreams and aspirations.

I know numerous parents who are primarily concentrated on their kids' needs, and often neglect their own well-being. If this resonates with you, keep in mind that your stress impacts your children as well. Several studies indicate that parents of children with autism face greater stress compared to parents of typically developing children. Many of us are strongly urged to act as both a parent and an autism therapist. I would say that's how it was for me, within the home. Research indicates that parents under high stress struggle more with adhering to their children's behaviour plans and executing autism interventions. This situation is detrimental for everyone involved.

'JACKIE' from Birmingham said, "My biggest challenge was too many parents believing their child has ADHD because they may get "too" hyperactive at times. ADHD is a proven chemical imbalance which can have a detrimental effect on the individual, but with so many diagnoses being handed out, this leaves the ones truly affected not being taken seriously."

In May 2023, a recent investigation by Lizzie Roberts in the *Telegraph* was uncovered that private clinics were prescribing strong medications for ADHD without conducting a proper diagnosis.

Patients and whistle-blowers have expressed worries about the hasty and subpar quality of online evaluations in certain private clinics. Official statistics indicate that the number of individuals receiving treatment for attention deficit hyperactivity disorder (ADHD) has surged by 80% over the past five years.

My challenges with my son's ADHD – food, nutrition, and diet

I feel nutrition plays a crucial role in life whether one has ADHD or autism spectrum disorder. For my son, who has been diagnosed with both, I prioritized his diet above everything else. He had a particular fondness for Haribo sweets, ready salted Pringles, Jaffa Cakes and fizzy drinks, all which significantly increased his energy levels and hyperactivity. I worked to replace these treats with fruit and low sugar foods, consistently trying to incorporate vegetables into most of his meals. Now at 11 years old and in senior school, during a growth spurt that has seen him reach the height of six-feet, I've noticed that he enjoys his food. My role as a parent has been to guide him towards a balanced diet. This has often been a challenge because while I can influence what he eats at home, it's during school hours and breaks that he tends to stop off at the local shop for cans of fizzy drinks, energy beverages, and packs of sweets if he didn't find the school dinners very appetising.

Research indicates that a high intake of fruits and vegetables may aid in reducing issues related to inattention. In a large study, researchers gathered information from parents of 134 children exhibiting ADHD symptoms through a comprehensive questionnaire about their typical dietary habits, including portion sizes, over a span of 90 days. Additionally, another questionnaire asked parents to assess their children's inattention symptoms, which are characteristic of ADHD, including struggle with focus, following instructions, remembering tasks, and managing emotions. The results revealed that children who consumed larger quantities of fruit and vegetables exhibited less severe inattention symptoms. The study also explored the effectiveness of a vitamin and mineral supplement containing 36 different ingredients for alleviating ADHD symptoms and emotional control issues. Findings indicated that children took the micronutrient supplement for their ADHD symptoms and emotional dysregulation.

As I conducted more research, I found that my understanding of ADHD and autism deepened significantly. I discovered a film titled *The Disruptors*. This documentary centres on families who have members with ADHD, showcasing their struggles and triumphs to help change the perception of ADHD and acknowledge its potential as a strength rather than just a disorder. My overall impression was one of astonishment and enlightenment; while there are many well-known personalities who have openly discussed their ADHD and autism, I believe there aren't enough films or documentaries that raise awareness about ADHD/autism spectrum disorders. Additionally, what I gained from watching *The Disruptors* was an understanding of how others cope with ADHD/autism in their day-to-day lives.

In my opinion, it's an excellent film; numerous reviews on IMDb are quite remarkable as many highlight the effect the movie had on them. One viewer went on to say, "Without a doubt the most outstanding documentary on ADHD. This documentary was a blessing and significantly helped our family for years. We have felt isolated and judged regarding ADHD, and this film has freed us to understand that we are not alone and that there are indeed positive aspects to ADHD. It's crucial for society to recognise the talents of these creative individuals and it's essential for school leaders to educate their teaching staff about the realities of this diagnosis so that children are not unfairly treated for a condition that is neuro-genetic and neuro-developmental. This documentary is heartfelt and finally sheds light on the truth surrounding this diagnosis, I would suggest it to both kids and parents. It's the film we have all been anticipating and it's viewed globally."

Another described the documentary as "skilfully produced" and conveys the truths, rather than the misconception, regarding one of the most prevalent mental health disorders.

This film was not only heart-wrenching and emotionally powerful, but it was also factual, sincere, and incredibly informative about the "actual scientific truths" surrounding this difficult condition. The film highlighted both the obstacles faced and the positive aspects of living with this neuro-disorder. Witnessing the struggles of the children featured in this film was truly enlightening. And my hope is that parents with children experiencing this condition can gain greater sense of compassion and understanding. I wish that kids who relate to this disorder can find some comfort in acknowledging that their challenges are valid and feel more empowered by recognising their strengths and harnessing them. I absolutely loved this movie and the whole concept.

ADHD can possess numerous beneficial characteristics, such as creativity, vigour, and resilience. These qualities can serve as a wellspring of motivation and inspiration. Creativity involves thinking unconventionally linking ideas in original ways and contributing distinctive viewpoints in creative fields. Energy and enthusiasm reflect a natural passion for living and can act as a source of motivation and encouragement for others.

Resilience is developed through overcoming obstacles, fostering perseverance and adaptability. Utilising humour to navigate challenging circumstances is part of the resilience. Hyperfocus allows individuals to accomplish remarkable tasks at a rapid pace when genuinely captivated. It also entails being deeply engrossed in a specific activity, often for long durations. Additional positive characteristics include determination, a sense of adventure, curiosity, strong intuition, effective conversational skills, spontaneity, social emotional abilities and advanced cognitive skills.

By the age of 12, my son had reached height of six-foot-two. Although he was a healthy six feet, and he maintained a slim build instead of being overweight, he still exhibited signs of both ADHD and autism, and at school he was provided with a time out pass allowing him to take a break or leave the classroom if he began to feel anxious or found the classroom environment overwhelming. This was implemented effectively and without delay, yet his teacher often reported that he was using his pass to wander off and disrupt other students in different classrooms, at times exceeding the agreed upon duration of his breaks. When confronted about his behaviour, he frequently responded that he didn't understand why he was acting that way and didn't quite understand the nature of the pass, which became another issue that arose over the following months. This behaviour impacted my son's ability to join school trips, causing him to miss out on these opportunities because his actions did not align with the expected standards.

However, after months of consistent effort in teaching my son the importance of accountability and setting clear expectations both at home and school, we observed significant improvements. I was so relieved to see him begin to take responsibility for his actions and behaviour improvements meant he was trusted to join his classmates on school excursions. He truly enjoyed himself, and I could see a sense of joy in him upon returning from his geography trip, where he engaged in an exploration of Birmingham. He gained a lot of knowledge and had a wonderful experience, although he did find the extensive walking challenging, as his legs often ached after prolonged periods without a break or stretch due to his dyspraxia. His teacher expressed satisfaction with his engagement and interest in the subject matter.

I believe that being the parent of a child with ADHD and autism spectrum disorders means continuously learning and striving for answers amid a fluctuating level of stress. I tend to check class charts with caution, sometimes apprehensive about the daily reports, yet I view class charts as a beneficial tool, as they enable parents to grasp how their child is performing throughout the school day with daily records from the lessons he participated in.

I had a conversation with a dear friend, who opened to me about the difficulties she encountered. I hold a great deal of respect for her after witnessing her firsthand battle with her son's spectrum disorders

'CATHERINE' from the Birmingham said, "My son was diagnosed with autism, SPD, ODD, anxiety and an extra clinical diagnosis of PDA with possible ADHD. From the age of 12 months old it was clear he had differences, although very forward in milestones for his age, his behaviour, emotionally and physically, was noticeable. We were fobbed off with the fact his father is serving a IPP sentence in prison and this was excused for his behaviours. Finally, on formal, diagnosis we had no support from school or paediatric specialists and the behaviour was very hard to deal with, however we refused medication on the basis of side effects and also not wanting to change my son's huge personality which the meds are known to do. Now he is almost 20, I question if that was always the right decision, however he's turned his life around in many ways. He still has his emotional struggles and ways of coping can still be hard, but he's now working full-time and about to be a dad for the first time."

Mirror traits of ADHD/autism disorders

1. Impulsive vs imaginative

2. Fidgety, unsettled, lively

3. Struggles to focus vs recognises links others overlook

4. Chaotic vs unplanned

5. Obstinate vs determined, resilient

6. Erratic vs demonstrates bursts of genius

7. Irritable vs compassionate

Approximately one in 57 children in the UK, or 1.76% are identified as being on the autism spectrum, which is considerably more than earlier estimates indicated. These findings come from a study involving over seven million children, conducted by researchers from the University of Cambridge's department of psychiatry in partnership with colleagues from Newcastle University. The highest prevalence was found among pupils of black ethnicity at 21%, while Roma/Irish travellers had the lowest at 0.85%, marking the first estimates for these groups. Students with an autism record in schools were 60% more likely to experience social disadvantages and 36% less likely to be English speakers. These results highlight notable variations in autism prevalence as documented within official educational systems. Based on ethnic backgrounds and geographical areas, Black and Chinese students had a 26% and 38% higher likelihood of being diagnosed with autism, respectively, and autistic children were considerably more prone to experiencing severe social disadvantages. These findings are reported today in *JAMA Paediatrics*.

I wanted to understand if ADHD/autism spectrum disorder was hereditary or if it was common in my family, being from such a large family with ten brothers and four sisters. I discovered that at least a cousin or a nephew or niece in my family had symptoms of ADHD/autism.

Someone I love and cherish deeply is my **AUNTY IVY**; while growing up I often watched her handle her son, who is on the autism spectrum, with great calmness. She shared, "When he was four, he used to spin a coat hanger as a way to relieve his stress. Although he still does it privately now that's he's older, some of the main challenges began when he was diagnosed at nine. He exhibited a lot of hyperactivity and unpredictability in his behaviour. He tends to keep to himself and was reluctant to interact. Even when surrounded by friends and family. I think he has a hard time socialising. It wasn't that he didn't want to; he just didn't know how. I would worry whenever he went out, as he faced teasing and didn't know how to respond. However, through years of constant reassurance, he has learnt to manage certain confrontations more efficiently. My biggest concern now, at 28, is his dependence on me for affection and stability, which can impact on my personal life. He feels uncomfortable when he sees me receiving affection from someone else or when it seems like I was giving more time to them than him. He is very polite has good manners and enjoys the home-cooked meals I prepare for him every day. Even though he still shows symptoms at 28, he has become more confident and more self-aware, more outgoing and motivated in his life over the years, which brings not only me but himself a lot of joy."

I contacted numerous individuals to gather their detailed experiences and was taken aback by the number of responses from those eager to contribute to my book and the topic. One noteworthy individual that had reached out to me was a guy named '**JAKE**' from Hackney. So that I could gain insight into how he manages his ADHD symptoms, I arranged a telephone call when it was suitable for him to share his experiences, and this is what he shared: "Eventually I accepted my ADHD and focused on challenging it by going to the gym and surrounding myself with positive influences. After experiencing a series of legal troubles due to hanging with the wrong crowd, I was placed in a special school for children with behavioural and learning challenges where I became a reflection of my surroundings. However, now that I have gained more insight, I strive to improve. Over the years I have come to understand myself better and find clarity in my life. Previously I would conceal my ADHD, feeling ashamed of being different, but I now have learned to accept it and almost see it as a badge of honour. I believe there is strong need for more support, less stigma, and greater outreach efforts for parents and young individuals."

He also added that he is currently finalising details to launch his new podcast show! "I have developed a strong desire to assist the next generation, whether through counselling or community support," said Jake.

My name is 'RACHEL', I am from Birmingham, and I have a 15-year-old daughter who has ASD and ADHD. From my experience there is little help once diagnosed. I had to fight for 2 years to get an EHCP to get my daughter into a school to meet her needs, now she is excelling at school, passing GCSE's a year before her peers and all because she is at a school who understands her needs, while it has been a challenge, it was worth the fight to get what my daughter deserves.

'REBECCA' from London expressed:

I am a mum to a 17yr old son with high functioning autism. He is amazing, kind, friendly and funny. He is passionate about what he loves and is an inspiration to others to be who they are and follow their dreams.

It has not been easy for him. Although I knew from around the age of two he was autistic, He was not diagnosed until the age 11 because academically he is very intelligent. But socially and emotionally he is immature which has affected his mental health and bonding with his peers. As his mum it has been sad to see and I have wanted to always step in and make things better but knowing that I have to let him figure it out himself has been a challenge for him as well as me.

There is support out there for many children with noticeable signs of autism and ehcp plans as they are funded for this. However, when they are doing well academically, they are left to it and struggle with their mental health as they are aware of their differences and feel they are not acccepted because of this. My son does not like to say he is autistic or talk about it in fear of being judged. Thankfully we as a society are becoming more aware of autism.

Autism is very much grouped into sections for practitioners, teachers and others to understand, however I have always said each child with autism is uniquely different from the next and the only person who truly knows them and what living with autism is like, are their parents/carers.

I have suggested to create parent groups to encourage social interactions with other high functioning autistic children like transport journeys or Minecraft/Lego building days, but it seems we keep to ourselves and struggle alone.

I worry what the big world will be like for him once he becomes an adult and makes his own decisions. I just hope he follows his passions, people are kind to him as he is to them, and he comes to me if and when needed.

I also want to add I do not like that they have named it high or low functioning autism. Should have stuck with autism and Asperger's. As I feel it can be seen as we are grading them. But that's just my feeling on it. I hope all children and adults with autism find their happy place!

Single dad 'LEE' 34 yrs old from Birmingham shared with me:

After my partner and I separated, I took on the responsibility of raising our son. When he was 8 his behaviour at times was challenging and hard to predict, which led to numerous disagreements between his mother and me. Eventually after a few years she decided it would be best for me to move out, allowing our son to live with me. Now 3 years him now being 11 he still has occasional unpredictable moments but his outbursts are much more controlled at home and at school. It's on ongoing effort! In summary! I believe that love, attention, support, patience, encouragement and a consistent routine, has been crucial to his development and continue to play a vital role in his progress!

Speaking to my friend '**SARAH**' from Birmingham she expressed:

My son struggled through the early years at school with the disorder and so did I as his mother. when he was about 10, he was first diagnosed with Add/Autism! he had always struggled with maintaining focus in class taking effective notes and recording his homework assignments. He often took a considerable about of time to get started on his work! Frequently submitted homework late and sometimes even when he had completed it he either forget to hand it in or miss placed it! Additionally, he was overly talkative which tended to distract his classmates, his performances were inconsistent and would achieve good results if he had a genuine interest in the subject but found it absolutely difficult to engage especially if he didn't like the teacher! Or the material he regularly came to class unprepared or disinterested, his teachers had never indicated that their might have been an underlying issue contributing to these challenges.

'**DON DON**' From London said, "It's incredibly frustrating when the education system fails to recognize the unique challenges faced by girls with ADHD, often treating them as if they were boys with the same condition. This lack of understanding and support can be draining, especially when teachers and schools lack the funding or experience to address the emotional struggles that come with ADHD in girls. Rather than seeing ADHD as a curse, it's important to recognize the blessings it can bring, such as fostering free thinking and strong self-love. When a child is written off as naughty simply because they are frustrated and not receiving the help they need, it sets them up for failure and perpetuates a cycle of discouragement."

'**SHANTY**' from Derby said:

A Mothers perspective

Having a child with ADHD can be overwhelming, can't it? The constant struggle to understand their mind, the guilt of not being patient and calm, the exhaustion of explaining and advocating... it's a lot to take in.

The public meltdowns, the stares, the whispers... it's like they're judging you, judging your child, judging your parenting. And those thoughts creep in - am I doing enough? Am I doing it right? The sleepless nights, the endless worrying... it's a heavy load.

And then there's the labels - 'naughty child', 'difficult kid'... like that's all they see. But you know what? Those labels are wrong. They're so wrong.

Because my child, my amazing child, is so much more than his ADHD. He is loving, he is kind, he is creative, and he is confident. He lights up a room, he makes friends everywhere, and he notices the little things that others miss.

And you know what? That's what's important. Not the labels, not the struggles, but the love, the laughter, and the adventures.

To all the parents out there, I see you. I know it's tough, but you're doing better than you think. Your child is blessed to have you, and they're going to grow up to be amazing.

And to my child, I say this: you are unique, you are fearfully and wonderfully made, and you are loved. ADHD is a part of who you are, but it doesn't define you. You are so much more than this. You are my everything.

'GARY':

I successfully organized and conducted a remarkable telephone interview with an individual named GARY S, whom I know from my previous college in Birmingham. We frequently discussed this topic during our classes, and he was more than willing to share his experiences to assist others. **'GARY'** stated: from a young age, I felt an extraordinary level of energy, surpassing that of the average person my age. At times, my mind resembled a fast-moving car; I was often labelled as hyperactive, disruptive, mischievous, and unpredictable. However, my parents informed me that I possessed a unique ability. When I inquired about its meaning, my mother explained that I had a mind capable of accomplishing tasks ten times over within the same hour! Initially, I was astonished, as my imagination conjured images of superheroes like Superman, Spider-Man, and He-Man. I wondered how incredible it would be to fly and scale walls with webs, wielding power with a mere gesture. Yet, my special abilities manifested as my creative thoughts, which intertwined and ignited with life. My mother advised me never to perceive this as a weakness. From the age of four, I struggled to remain still, articulate my thoughts clearly, and often threw objects without provocation. When instructed to cease, I would continue with a smile, treating it as a game. My mother noted that I found it challenging to distinguish between what constituted naughty behavior and acceptable conduct. As I transitioned into my teenage years, I realized that we are all inherently driven by movement and action, even when it feels as though the world is attempting to restrain me. My focus would shift into high gear, a phenomenon they referred to as hyper-focus. To my understanding, this occurs when one is passionate about something, leading to impulsive behavior in the pursuit of excellence. At times, I would become engrossed in my thoughts, feeling invincible. I noticed details that others overlooked, and my mind connected concepts rapidly, which also instilled a sense of fearlessness in me. I approached life with enthusiasm, rarely overthinking my actions. I now perceive myself as a distinct type of powerful individual! Thank you, Owen, for providing me with the opportunity to share my story! May God bless you, Gary S.

Sourced online from the rapper 'GIGGS':

ADHD-Autism has a globally effect on society!

People with ADHD /Autism face higher risks of accidents, substance use, and early mortality, alongside challenges in academic and professional life. While the prevalence varies by region, gender, and age, it is a persistent global issue affecting approximately 2.5% of children and 5% of adults.

Rapper Giggs has recently spoke out about his battle with ADHD and how he was able to overcome it with music , where he has gone on to be a hip hop legend,and rap icon for the UK rap scene!

Childhood Struggles: He described being frequently kicked out of class for "answering back" and feeling misunderstood by teachers and peers. He spent time alone in the playground and felt people his age were immature. This lack of understanding led him to believe he was inherently "bad," a mindset he carried into adulthood.

Impact on Life: He credits music with saving his life, stating that before his career took off, his path led to two prison sentences.

Advocacy: He now advocates for better support for neurodivergent children, highlighting the difficulties his own children face in securing necessary Education, Health and Care Plans (EHCPs) within the current system.

Awareness and Pride: Giggs aims to challenge the stigma around autism, encouraging others with the condition to embrace their talents and see themselves as "gifted, special". He released a song with his son, ML, called "Own Motion," which explores their shared experiences of struggling to fit in.

I have so much admiration and respect for Giggs for using his public figure to speak out and spread awareness to a disorder that is so often overlooked and un-nurtured in our society!

Rapper 'BUGZY MALONE' also recently opened up about his experiences with ADHD on a radio interview with capital FM:

Bugzy Malone expressed: I have a superpower, it's my Adhd it's the way my brain works! At school the teachers often referred to him as having a disorder because he learns different from the other kids in school, he went on to say he never finished school and by the age of 16 he was sat in jail! So he had to figure out how his brain worked , he said from the moment he wakes up his mind is automatically focused on a few different things , a little bit of everything every day with a main vision and said he had could already see where he was heading , knew how it was going to look, but was just a little unsure in to how he was going to get there in fact he said that he felt (quote) "Unconventional" into how he was going to do it

He said he only focuses on the positive aspects of his ADHD and don't tend to focus to much on the negative conclusions and refuses to make society persuade him that he has a disorder or that there's something wrong with him!

Bugzy Malone has since gone on to win MOBO Award for best grime act, multiple Uk top 10 Ep Albums viral Success with 100 million views and received an inaugural "B.inspired" award! For his contributions and reviving of the Manchester music grime scene and also a clothing line and a successful acting role.

I have much respect to Bugzy Malone for sharing his experiences with ADHD to his fans and audience as it's not easy to open up about sensitive experiences but I admire his dedication and determination to combat his spectrums with hard work and positive thought and you can too!

I aimed to investigate various disorders and spectrums during my journey, not only to enhance my own understanding but also to enlighten others. One condition I encountered was Savant Autism. I discovered two intriguing documentaries on YouTube featuring Stephen Wilkshire and Flo and Kay Lyman, who were individuals living with this condition.

'FLO AND KAY LYMAN TWINS'

According to reports flo and Kay are the only female autistic savant twins in the world. What is remarkable is that the twins' talents and traits are nearly identical. They possess the ability of calendar calculation, a mental condition that enables them to recall the weather and every meal they have consumed for almost every day of their lives. Family members described them as friendly and very engaging, yet many labeled them as mentally retarded. This illustrates the pressing need for greater understanding and education regarding ADHD, Autism, and ADD. The twins were diagnosed as autistic savants, a condition where an individual with mental disabilities exhibits an extraordinary talent in a specific area, typically mathematics, music, or art. During their childhood, Flo and Kay's abilities went unrecognized and misunderstood, resulting in years of undiagnosed conditions. Their parents feared societal stigma and were apprehensive about being blamed for their daughters' condition, which contributed to their reluctance to seek help due to the embarrassment they felt. Flo and Kay faced significant ridicule, struggling to make friends and fit in, particularly during high school and in their community. They endured severe abuse, bullying, and name-calling. Their mother often confined them to their rooms, displaying signs of difficulty in coping and at times appearing to reject them. Overall, the twins' condition was grossly misunderstood, especially in the 1960s when obtaining a diagnosis was considerably more challenging. The twins frequently referred to themselves as human computers. The experiences of many, particularly those with Autism, can be incredibly perplexing due to the numerous challenges associated with these conditions. Flo and Kay utilized crayons to create charts detailing their favourite celebrities' outfits on television and the weather on specific days, as they faced numerous sensory issues, including heightened levels of sensory perception and touch. At times, their senses did not function in

'STEPHEN WILKSHIRE'

I encountered numerous fascinating articles and documentaries about a young man named "Stephen Wilkshire." One documentary that particularly stood out for its depth and educational value is titled "Billions of Windows" featuring Stephen Wilkshire, which can be found on YouTube. Stephen was born in 1974 in London and has severe autism. As a consequence of his condition, he was mute until the age of five, during which time he could not communicate verbally. He turned to alternative forms of expression, such as drawing. As a child, he was constantly sketching everything from animals to people. By the age of eight, he had discovered his niche in drawing buildings. He is regarded as a unique landscape artist. After a single flight over New York City during a 20-minute helicopter ride, he produced an intricate cityscape drawing on a 19-foot canvas, demonstrating astonishing accuracy solely from his memory. He also created notable cityscapes of Tokyo and Rome. He is recognized for his remarkable ability to depict landscapes from memory after observing them just once. Stephen was diagnosed with savant syndrome, a condition where individuals with significant mental disabilities exhibit certain abilities that far exceed the average. The skills associated with savant syndrome typically relate to memory and may also encompass rapid mental calculations, artistic talent, musical skills, or cartography. After conducting research on YouTube and various other media articles, I sought to determine the average market value of some of Stephen's drawings. Following some impressive reviews, I discovered a piece of work that Stephen created on an A0-sized drawing, depicting a landscape of Marina Bay in Singapore, which sold for an astonishing £47,800! I found this truly remarkable, and it illustrated to me that ADHD and Autism spectrums can be perceived as a form of superpower, depending on the individual's mindset. Through extensive research, I have found that many people view Autism and

ADHD spectrums as a disorder of the mind; however, I tend to disagree. I perceive it more as a condition of the individual's mind, acknowledging that all traits associated with ADHD and Autism are entirely different in terms of experiences, effects, and coping mechanisms.

Conclusion

This is my second book that I have written in a year; I've been extremely driven to complete it even while dealing with various challenges in life. Though I was good at maths in school, I struggled to maintain focus for extended periods unless the topic genuinely interested me, which helped me stay engaged and connected to my classroom settings. After doing thorough research and having a son on the spectrum, along with hearing friends and others talk about their experiences with managing ADHD/autism or raising a child with these traits, I've realised that I might show signs of ADHD myself at 44 years old. My next step is to get an assessment and follow the required process while I wait for results from a specialist. My primary goal for my book is to bring awareness to those who feel isolated and lack answers or support regarding ADHD/autism spectrum disorders, whether it's due to insufficient information or for first-time moms or parents/single parents who feel overwhelmed with worry, stress, anxiety.

I hope my book can serve as a source of guidance, if not reassurance, along with the techniques I use with my son that might also be beneficial, and stories from others sharing their life challenging experiences on dealing with ADHD/autism spectrums. God bless and thank you.

All I ask is that you leave an honest review on my Amazon review page; manners and respect are much appreciated.

Onelove
Author Element OG
Owen Williams